Lynnie Godfrey

Sharing Lessons Learned While Seeking the Spotlight

Blue Heron Book Works, LLC

Allentown, Pennsylvania

ISBN: 0-9968177-5-1
ISBN-13: 978-0-9968177-5-2
Cover design by Angie Zambrano
Cover photo by Lori Smith 2015
Caricature sketch on cover by Sam Norkin

Blue Heron Book Works, LLC
Allentown, Pennsylvania
www.blueheronbookworks.com

Contents

ACKNOWLEDGMENTS

I first want to thank God for always knowing what was best for me. Thank You for always giving me what I needed as opposed to what I *wanted* and probably could not have handled.

Secondly, I want to thank my small nuclear family for their unconditional faith in me as I "seek the spotlight." Thank you, Maggie and Fred Godfrey (my parents), Jo-Ann Wood, Lossie Godfrey (my Nana) and Uncle Mike "Betsy" Stephens (my Grand Uncle).

Thank you to Brian Bechel, Mark Westlund, Brenda Pressley, Nina Reehl and my sweet Celeste Bedford Walker for being my test bunnies and listening boards for this and all other projects.

And finally I would like to acknowledge my husband of more than three decades, Carl E. Lee. Thank you for your support, accurate criticism, insight and foresight and always being there to "Drive Miss Daisy" whether it was by car or spirit...you have been an inspiration and an example of a dedicated, supportive husband who has not chosen to throw me away …. Yet!

Note:
By the way all you naysayers…the lovely cover photo by Lori Smith was taken on the hundredth anniversary of my father's birthday, November 3, 2015. It is a recent photo, thank you… The sketch by Sam Norkin was done almost thirty years ago.

INTRODUCTION

My wonderful editor Bathsheba Monk asked an interesting question the other day. "Why," she asked "are you writing these particular stories?" The answer that immediately jumped into my head was to "to help somebody."

"If I Can Help Somebody" was my Mother's favorite song. She sang it often as a soloist in church and even at funerals. Yes, my beautiful mother was a singer. It is an old hymn maybe gospel but for sure religious and it talks about helping someone "so my living won't be in vain." That might sound dramatic and maybe it is but that is what comes to mind. My family, the nucleus in which I was born and raised, my parents Fred and Maggie Godfrey, my "Nana," Lossie Godfrey, my Great Uncle Mike "Betsy" Stephens and most recently this year my dear sweet sister/cousin Jo-Ann Wood have all gone now. I am an only child once again and I want to use my time now honoring their memory and helping others by sharing the benefit of my experience and knowledge.

There are other lovely relatives that remain: Larry Wood, Kenneth Gainer, the two Delores's—Baker and Bolden— as well as a host of friends who are like family: lifelong pal (since the age of 3 or 5) Gail Madison Burris and high school friends Deborah Fudge Rhem and her sister Sondra Fudge Thornton. I feel blessed to have all you wonderful people. But my nucleus is gone and "so I want *my* living to not be in vain." I want this guide to help people from all walks of life to see that there is a need to stay on the path. Opportunity always knocks—yes, it does and often repeatedly!—and one must be ready to take its call, no matter what field you pursue. My field is performing and so in a sense I had more practice perhaps than other people in being "on." In show business, you're always ready because you never know who's in the audience that night, who's turned the dial to your network performance on a whim, so you're always giving it your best. But the same holds true for all walks of life for people who want to succeed: you never know if someone watching is looking for someone with exactly your talents. When the door opens you must be prepared—energy up! performance high!—to walk through and wow them!

Because my life in show business has taken me on so many different rides, the term "bravery" comes up a lot when people ask me about my career. "Lynnie, you are so brave to tackle such a challenge." That always surprises me, because I think that "Necessity is the Mother of Invention." I had to go out and do the things I did. No one would discover me in my mother's living room. The other reason: I wanted to test myself and my limits.

What a blessing to have had the support system that I had in my aforementioned nucleus family and now have in my husband, Carl E. Lee. In fact, looking back on it, I realize I am always working with a net of love and support and I know that that is not available to everyone so you have to be persistent and resilient and never give up faith in yourself. That is your job: I charge you to believe in *you*!

If you are reading this, I think you already believe in yourself and feel the fire burning inside yourself but you want to know how to get from point A—singing in your mother's living room—to point B, which is taking a bow in front of a standing ovation.

As you will read in this book, though, there is no magic formula to get from point A to point B. There isn't even a "best route." This is life, not Google Maps, baby! There are certain things you can control and lots you can't. And sometimes you will take the "wrong" path at the fork in the road and find yourself in a dark forest thinking, "how the heck did I get here?" without a visible way out. But just maybe—if you keep walking—you'll find yourself at another right place. Or even a better place. Yes, that happens *all* the time. I want to give you the benefit of my experiences and knowledge of the business to help you nail the things you can control, and eventually the things you can't control—those doors of opportunity—will start opening for you.

These tidbits of my life can apply to anyone doing anything. So read about my little ride in life. I have chosen some stories I thought might interest and help you without hurting anyone else. Oh, are there stories that could hurt? Oh *yesssss*. But that is another book…that we'll talk about later.

"IT DON'T MEAN A THING IF IT AIN'T GOT THAT SWING"

This is a great line from the fabulous Edward Kennedy Ellington known as "Duke." It's a song I cover, too, in my cabaret performances.

As with all great lines, it can mean many things to different people. But to me it always meant: if it's not special, why are you doing it? If you don't love it, how do you expect anyone else to love it? "Swing" is that extra zing that fuels the ride, that extra fillip that combined with your own talent and zest makes magic, that makes you memorable, that makes people want more!

"Swing" isn't fairy dust, though. It's based on a strong foundation of support, a burning desire and lots of practice and self-knowledge of your own talents. Swing is artistry combined with lots of hard work and honest feed-back from people who want you to succeed.

A Strong Foundation of Support

I can't tell you often or strongly enough how important it is to have people rooting for you, believing in you, mentoring you…people who have your back, because

4

here's a secret you can write down: no one succeeds on their own.

I was lucky to have the unconditional love and support of two of the most wonderful people on the planet: my parents. This is a simple story, because the people were simple. My father, Fred "Buster" Godfrey was born one hundred years ago (1915) in Marianna, Florida to Lossie Stephens Godfrey and John Godfrey and my mother, Maggie Mae Wood Godfrey was born almost as many years ago (I still promise not reveal her real age!) to Emma Gainer Wood and George Wood in Panama City Florida. They met in Marianna, Florida while both worked in a hotel—Mother as a maid and Dad (or Pop as he would come to be called) was a cook. They courted and before Dad was drafted into World War II they married. After the war as he was being discharged my father insisted on moving to New York City. I think that migration was due to the extreme racism that my father experienced (as a young boy he watched from behind bushes as one of his good friends was lynched, a memory he never forgot or forgave).

The move north was fortuitous for me for that is where I was born many years and after five miscarriages later. They were ambitious in the best sense. They both learned trades and worked two jobs, they opened their own businesses and realized a dream of education and a better life for their child—me.

I am often told that my choices in life have displayed courage. I smile because the challenges that these two steadfast people faced make my choices seem wimpy at best. To come north knowing only her brother Lester and her childhood friend Myrtle Baker was incredibly brave for my mother and to find a place in Harlem in the apartment next to Myrtle for my father to come to after his discharge

5

was truly the sign of a person with an iron will.

My mother had lost her mother at the age of nine and raised her baby sister Eleanor (my sweet Jo-Ann's birth mother who died quite young) and three brothers, her eldest brother Lester, Carl, the middle brother and baby Wilbert all by herself. She lived to see all in her family precede her in death except Uncle Lester who died the day after my mother passed away.

A hard life of being pushed around to family members and abbreviated education were things my mother had to look forward to as an adolescent, however, she showed no signs of resentment or anger…she was by far the *best mother* ever! She passed on to me her dreams of performing. She sang on the radio early in life but stopped to raise me. She passed on her determination and strength of character. I hope I do her justice with my presence and carriage, but nothing that I do will come close to her youthful non-make-up beauty, and every day I look at my mother's youthful picture and see if I can match her beauty. No. Not ever. Can't match her beauty.

And then there is my father, Fred Godfrey. He was the oldest son of four children. His only sister was Pearline, the only girl who was very personable and whom, I am told, I resemble physically. She was another beauty who was lost to us too early. Aunt Pearline was out for a Sunday ride in one of those Model Ts and the driver was going too fast. The car turned over and somehow my aunt wound up partially under the car. My father was following in his vehicle, and through adrenalin he lifted the car off my aunt. Internal injuries were treated by a doctor (who was Black) but she needed more extensive treatment. Being Black, she was refused more extensive medical attention from the white hospital and she was dismissed and sent home. Eight months later in the home of my grandmother Lossie

Godfrey, she died. It was said she would sit up in the bed those eight months and greet her visitors (all of whom knew her fate) in full make-up and dressing gown. Theatrical don't you think? Maybe that is one of my sources of theatricality.

Sadly, all of my uncles on both sides of my parents succumbed to alcohol which I think accounts for the fact that I cannot stand the smell of it to this day.

My father passed on to me his elegance for dressing, his eloquence, as well as an unconditional integrity for self-respect which to this day will probably work for and against me in a business that relies heavily on insecurity and greed. He fought for his vision of racial freedom for me until the day he passed away.

And with all this, my parents went on to own their own businesses, property and live lovely lives. I miss them every day. Fifty one years of marriage. My father passed away from complication of an abdominal aneurysm and my mother passed away 2 ½ years later from a broken heart. I believe in broken hearts.

Their dream for a small child who knew the word "college" at the age of three but did not know what it meant has come true in many ways. They saw many dreams come true right before their eyes and I am grateful for that.

Nothing I have faced in my life comes close to the things my parents had to deal with, so whenever courage or bravery is mentioned I have a great reference base.

My parents gave me the base I'm talking about. They supported me while I grew.

Friends

As crucial as supportive parents and family are, the people who will shore you up every day are your friends and colleagues. I would say that even if you didn't have the comfortable net of loving supportive parents that I had, it's possible to make up for it with a loving network of true friends.

Of course the question is: How do you know the people you are surrounding yourself with are true friends?

About three days after the first twitter for the publication for this effort appeared, I started getting Facebook messages from some highly visible people whom I had not heard from in a while. We are still friendly and the reason for us not communicating is simple: We are all busy. However, it eventually occurred to me (yes, I am slow) that some of my associates were concerned that I might be mentioning some of the experiences that we have shared. Well, there are those of you that will be disappointed because that is not, nor was it ever, the point of this book to be a tell-all my friends' "secrets" book. The people who were worried will be elated to know their secrets are and will always be safe with me.

That's the prime quality, in my opinion, of a true friend. Someone who will be loyal to the end. Someone who will keep your secrets—and by secrets I mean those times that maybe you weren't your best self. They will keep your secrets because they care about you and they also know if they show another person in a not-so-flattering light those doors of opportunity I was talking about will start slamming. It actually works both ways, of course. The doors will start slamming in the face of the person you betrayed—yes, betrayed!—but they will slowly but surely start closing in your face as well. No one likes to associate with people who aren't loyal for obvious reasons: if you "told all" about one person, you will more than likely do it to someone else. And people stay clear.

So, your first task in creating a network of friends is to

find people who will not betray you. Surround yourself with them. And the way to attract those people to you is to be a person who will not betray others! Pretty simple!

Your next job is to find people who you not only trust, but who have gone where you want to go or who have knowledge that you want.

My Personal Network

I always work better with men. I think my father wanted a boy and gave me some masculine values that sometimes clash with women.

I'm the only woman I know who loves Westerns. *Red River* starring Montgomery Cliff and John Wayne is my favorite, I hum the theme all the time. Then comes the Rick Nelson, Walter Brennan, Dean Martin and John Wayne film *Rio Bravo. El Dorado* is the somewhat-remake with John Wayne, Robert Mitchum and a very young James Caan.

I watch World War II war films all the time. I don't even have a favorite. I like them all.

And my personal network is made up of mostly men and I want to tell you the stories of what they meant to me and how they helped me.

But, I guarantee you this is not going to be the story you think it is going to be.

My personal heroes are my father Fred Godfrey, my Great Uncle Mike "Betsy" Stephens, and my "Uncle" Matthew Spires (married to my mother's cousin Johnnie Mae Wood Spires).

My professional heroes are my vocal teacher, Dr. Chauncey Northern, my acting and directing teacher, Lloyd Richards, musical genius, Eubie Blake, and writing and producing genius Norman Lear. That is a good list.

Both my personal and professional heroes have always supported me and inspired me by their actions, even when I wasn't in contact with them.

The Men in My Life: The Broadway Stories

I had done my time on tour and showcases in New York in churches and basements and then came an advertisement in the *Back Stage* and *Show Business Trade* papers. They were looking for a Vivian Reed type. I know Vivian and we are not alike. She is fabulous! But I went in anyway because they were looking for people who could sing the songs of the 20s, 30s and 40s: my kind of music. The name of the production was *Shuffle Along*. The audition was a breeze and they called almost immediately to offer me the job. That job changed my life.

Before *Shuffle Along* I had come close to getting to Broadway with a wonderful show called *Ragtime Blues* directed by casting legend Jay Binder and written by Mitch Douglas. It featured the music of ragtime pianist, Scott Joplin. It was this show where I met my life-long brothers Ken Page (of *Ain't MisBehavin'*, *The Wiz*, *Cats* and the film *Dreamgirls* fame), theater-legend Saundra Reeves Phillips, and Franz Jones (*Big River* on Broadway). We all still share a passion for this business and support each other to this day.

Ragtime Blues was received well but never got the financial backing it deserved and never moved to Broadway, however the showcase *Shuffle Along* was different. *Shuffle Along* was my first all-Black cast. It was received quite well. The show (and I) got wonderful notices. Opening night in the ninety seat house of the now defunct 33rd Street theatre Theatre-Off-Park was a special night for another reason too. That was the night that I met the legendary Eubie Blake. As the lights were lowered he said in the dark to the entire audience so we all backstage could hear, "Now we are all the same color." A memorable line after all these years later.

The cast of *Shuffle* was four people: Dabriah Chapman, Vernon Spencer, Roger Lawson, and me. We all did fine work. I was asked to do the backers audition all by myself and, after the finances were secured, I was asked to be a part of the Broadway production. This new production would be called *EUBIE!* The cast would expand to include the great Alaina Reed (Hall), the incredible Gregory Hines and absolute consummate dancer Lonnie McNeil; all three have since passed away. Here are the members that remain with us: Maurice Hines Jr., Mel Johnson Jr., Jeffery V. Thompson, Janet Powell, Ethel Beatty, Marion Ramsey, Leslie Dockery and me. We started out of town with this cast. During the out of town run, performances by then-understudy Terry Burrell were so phenomenal that she was asked to join the cast and finished out the membership of the original Broadway production.

We had many understudies, but David Jackson, Carol Mallard, Jackie Lowe, Andrea Frierson, and Bernard Marsh were our family and were there from the beginning. Wonderful performers.

The highlight of this whole experience was meeting and knowing Eubie Blake. He was so proud I had made it to Broadway having been in the original showcase for the show, and he and his lovely wife Marion became my good friends, attending my wedding and gifting my husband Carl and me with Tiffany money that I still treasure in my bank vault. Eubie also came over to our table at the wedding, accompanied by producer Ashton Springer, and brought several hundred dollar bills to add to the gift that he and Marion had already given us. He was a generous man in every sense. What wonderful people and wonderful memories. What a great run.

I remember walking down the street with Gregory Hines after one of our soirees during the Broadway run of *EUBIE!* I was nearing the end of the run and everyone was planning their next move, everyone that is but me. I was tired. I had done the showcase, the backers auditions and then the entire run of the show, and I wanted and needed a break. But not the indomitable Gregory. He had a plan about what he had to do next. He was always in a hurry for the next project. Sometimes I think he thought he had to cram everything into the time he had here. You see Maurice and Gregory were like brothers to me: they watched me grow in the show.

I watched them every night and learned so much from them. My performance was put in between Maurice's seductive *Got to Get the Gitten* and Gregory's tap phenomenon *Hot Feet* (where he controlled the audience's applause by saying "not yet, not yet"). My number was the female 11 o'clock number called *Cravin* done originally in 1921 by the incredible Florence Mills. The incredible performances of the Hines brothers forced me to try to bring the house down every night.

Gregory had introduced me to my husband and was best man at our wedding, so discussing what I was to do next seemed in a way his responsibility.

Gregory went on to do more Broadway while I took a break. I decided to pass on the National tour of *EUBIE!* to do what would become my signature for a while: Doing roles never or seldom done by a Black woman. I started with Lola of *Damn Yankees* at Hartford Stage. I understand it broke the box office record. In that production, my devil was the late brilliant Tony Award winner, David Rounds, and Joe was Tony Award winner Michael Rupert. What a role. What a great show. I would love to do it again, but the dancing could kill me! I went on to other challenges in the theatre after that. Always my men friends encouraged me to stretch, encouraged me to try.

The Men in My Life: The Hollywood Years

And then, I was ready to move. Broadway has yet to beckon again, maybe it will in the future, but then it was time to move to Hollywood.

Hollywood would be a challenge of reinvention. I had to soften my style, technique, and look. But that's not impossible for a trained thespian. I did commercials, a play, a Saturday Morning series, a recurring role on a prime time network show and over thirty guest shots.

One of my favorite gigs was playing Helen the Computer on *The New Monkees*. Here's how it started: my LA agent told me to go to an audition for a "Cybil Shepherd" type in a new animation Saturday morning series called *The New Monkees* The audition room was filled with blondes, I was the only exception. I did not let that deter me. I went in singing my song and reading my lines and won the part of Helen the Computer. They painted my lips red and painted my face green. What great fun it was to perform with that wonderful group of guys for a couple of seasons.

I thought I had enough experience to try to get on a network series. But that was not in the cards. I was always the second choice when "going to network" as it was called. It would eventually take one of the most powerful men in Hollywood to defend my talent and usher me into my first prime time television series as the female *lead* of a new series that was the sequel to one of the most successful situation comedies of all times: *All In The Family* the story of the Archie Bunker Family. Our series was titled *704 Hauser*, the address of the Archie Bunker family, and we were off like a bullet.

It started like this: I was in New York City doing a workshop of the Broadway bound Musical *39* about the wonderful music that was written in the fabulously creative year 1939. For me, it marked the end of an era. It was the first time my parents would not make it to a performance of mine. My mother was not feeling well, and my father was not comfortable coming without her. It was an omen I did not want to acknowledge: my safety net was fraying.

My New York agents got a call to put me on tape for the role of a neighbor for a new Norman Lear series. I thought to myself "here we go again" I had been flown by Mr. Lear almost a decade earlier to test for a series that never got done. (By the way, when I finally did get to work with Mr. Lear, he did not remember that first trip he had me flown to LA.) When Mr. Lear got to New York to audition those actors that interested him for the new series, I was in tech rehearsal for *39* and could not be released for the audition. I was disappointed but not devastated, after all I thought this product was going to Broadway and I was hoping I would be chosen to go with it. Fast forward: the production did not get picked up and I returned to LA for a six month stay for work. As soon as I arrived my agent said, "Norman Lear or rather the casting agent Reuben Cannon is looking for you." I was elated. They hadn't cast the plum role which was something like Jackée Harry's Sondra in *227*, a situation comedy I had previously worked on. A breakthrough role.

Well, as the fates would have it, that was not the role

Mr. Lear had in mind for me. He didn't want me for the secondary role but the primary role: the lead. Mr. Lear had changed his mind on a casting choice and decided to go in another direction. As I sat in the casting building in the long hall I was alone. No other actresses. Strange, I thought. Then suddenly there he was, the legendary Norman Lear in his trademark white hat and surrounded by an entourage of important looking people. As he approached I saw him turn and say something to one of the people in the entourage. I would later learn he said, "She is pretty. I sure hope she can act." Well, God was with me and act I did. I played my mother a strongly religious Pentecostal woman and a few hours later I got the call that Norman Lear has signed me to a contract.

The series did not play long on television for a number of reasons, but I bring it up because the circumstances around it and in my life were significant and influence me to this day.

A Hole in the Net

Wonderful, right? Things were breaking for me professionally. My personal network surrounded me like a suede glove, supporting me and cheering me on. But nothing stays the same forever.

At almost the same time my career in Hollywood was taking off, my dear father was not feeling well and the family learned almost immediately that he had an abdominal aneurysm that had to be operated on right away. Oh boy, Ying and Yang. I accepted the role in the series and then attended to my father every day in Beth Israel Hospital in New York. I drove my mother 50 miles round trip every day until the pilot was to be shot and I left my father for LA to shoot the most important piece of work in my career while one of the most important people in my life lay in a surgically induced coma. I checked with my family every day and every day he remained the same. No change.

We shot the pilot, both a great and nerve racking experience because of the circumstances. When we finished shooting I immediately flew back to New York. I was back a week when my Father regained consciousness and finally gained control of all of his faculties.

He was in intensive care for three months, but he was ready to come home. He wanted to come to my house. We all agreed I could watch him because my mother was too exhausted to do so. Within 24 hours at my home my father got a fever and died. To say I was devastated was an understatement. I went on to do the series, my mother even flew out to see me tape a couple of episodes, but nothing was the same again. Two years after that, with the series in the can and notice received that the series was not going any further, my life became taking care of my mother. My mother by that time was heart-broken at the passing of my father. I took her from Los Angeles back to my home in New Jersey where she spent her last Christmas with me and peacefully passed away in the very same room my father passed away in, in my home. I like to say it was a completion of a cycle. You see, my mother was the first person I saw when I came into this life and I was the last person she heard (I sang her favorite song) and saw before she passed.

When I say that I was blessed to have strong supportive parents as part of my foundation, it's true. What's also true is that when you lose that you have to build and rely on other support systems.

So, then it was up to me to go on and find a different

motivation to perform. Not easy. And the first place to look is within yourself.

Burning Desire

Every artistic career starts somewhere, usually in childhood with a burning desire.

I had a burning desire in childhood, but it was a burning desire to be a *math and English teacher*. Yes, I always had a good voice and, yes, as a young child I tapped on *Star Time*, a children's television show broadcast from New York City, but I imagined I could do those things on the weekend at nightclubs. During the week I would diagram sentences and do long division in front of a rapt audience of ten year olds!

Even on Children's Day—the Black community in Harlem where I was raised celebrated Children's Day in addition to celebrating Mother and Father's day—I was taken to the store (usually to our beloved 125th St. to buy from Black-owned businesses there) to pick out a present and I always picked out a chalk board and chalk. I would take it back to my room where my dolls were lined up in rows and I would teach!

I had singing lessons, but when it came time to pick out a college I picked Hampton University in Hampton, Virginia. But it was in a school play while there that I was introduced to the part of Sister Sonji by Sonia Sanchez a girl who was going to Hunter College, that I changed my direction from education to performing and the fire to perform was ignited in me. This is a case of life imitating art! After that experience, I realized that I missed the city and wouldn't it be good to go to Hunter College just like my character had? I had already been admitted to Hunter College so I reapplied and was quickly admitted—I was a

Dean's List student at Hampton—and decided I could be an education major there. I would be Nancy Wilson—my idol—on weekends.

I had also decided to perform, and the practical things was to study in New York City. Studying in New York City or any major city used to mean that you got the opportunity to study with the best. I don't think it does anymore. Students are not encouraged to work with or be mentored by professionals. Why? I don't know. Don't ask me. But I digress....

At Hunter College I registered for a Black Theatre History course that was to be given by an actor who had appeared quite briefly (now as a professional I believe he was probably a day player) in the film *Shaft*. However, when the class was about to start, in walked this diminutive man with a cane. He limped in and I had no idea who he was. I was smart enough to zero in on everyone's reaction to this man which was almost reverential. I thought I would drop the class, but I was curious so I took my ignorant a** up to the library to research who he was. There was no google then, believe me.

In this class on that very important day was another occurrence worth mentioning. It was my nineteenth birthday. I met lifelong friends Joy (it was Vicki then) Morton (Wiley), Debbie Austin, Brenda Thomas (Denmark), Miki Dash (Wilkinson) and Julius Hollingsworth. I'm still in contact with them or talk to them almost daily in the case of Joy and Julius.

So, in the library, I sat down and started to read about this man who was named Lloyd Richards. He was the first Black director on Broadway, directing the elite in theatre history: the brilliant and Oscar winning Sidney Poitier and both the brilliant and beautiful Diana Sands and Ruby Dee, Ossie Davis a talented actor, humanitarian, activist and writer and the incomparable Ms. Claudia McNeil, wonderful all. The play was none other than *A Raisin In The Sun!*

Needless to say I almost passed out and slapped my stupid self at the same time. That was a Monday. The class met three days a week. You better believe that by Wednesday Mr. Richards could not get rid of me, and I stayed at his side for the next two and half years as an intern/student. He and Vera Roberts, the chairman of the department, were my advisors and I studied acting and directing with him.

SOME BEGINNING!

After that I became a drama major with communications as my minor.

But it was watching Lloyd, his patience with students and actors and his passion for the arts that made me fall in love with the theater. And that's the burning passion that has fueled my career. But here's another secret to success in show business—write it down, please!—and that's versatility.

Be Prepared

Everyone wants to be an actor, of course, because it's the actors who get the recognition and the immediate approbation on the stage. There's nothing like applause! While Lloyd did have some early success as an actor—the role he spoke of most often was his Iago in *Othello*— eventually he started directing and his specialty became coaching performances out of other actors. He had a very calming way of coaxing the character through an actor.

Lloyd told me I had to take acting classes. And soon I

was in a play. My first play was when I was a junior. I played Cookie in *Postscript* by Geoffrey Steinhertz with Perry Smith and Dick Hitchcock. And I got my first review ever—in the *Hunter Envoy*, "Caroline Godfrey is a lovely lady with a lovely voice. She played Cookie with delicacy and compassion."

It was heady stuff!

Still, I'm a pragmatist. And when Lloyd advised me that there were only but so many roles written for Black women in the theater professionally and even in Hunter College. I listened and at his suggestion started to direct. I did Charles Fuller's play, *All's Fair*, in 1975 and Ossie Davis' musical *Purlie* in 1976. I am blessed to be able to sing and dance, and I knew if I could also act and direct, I would never be out of work in show business if I wanted it. The secret, I would find out later, was being able to shape my career, not just respond to opportunities other people presented to me—although I have always found that they do find you when you aren't looking.

As Lloyd always told me, "If you don't see it, create it!" When other people would say, "How come you got that, or how come you got this?" I would always tell them, there are plenty of opportunities out there for everyone. All you have to do is look. And, remember, if you don't see it, create it!

I think this is important to remember for young actors coming up. If you aren't from show biz royalty you have to find your own opportunities. You have to make people realize that your talent and your hard work are what bring people to the show, not just your name. Don't get me wrong. I came from the royalty of the Godfreys which means more than anything in the world to me—I never changed my name even when I got married—but it didn't open doors for me in the business. My hard-earned reputation opened the doors. It was my good fortune to receive good reviews.

As I was writing this book, my editor made me bring out all my reviews and I put them in big scrapbooks that my husband, Carl, bought me years ago. Before this, I never had reason to go back over my life—I am too busy going forward—and frankly I had forgotten a lot of performances and a lot of the great reviews I received over the years. My mother saved most of them, not me. My editor was more impressed than I was, however, and she said on more than one occasion as she was reading my press, "My God, haven't you ever gotten a bad review?" because truthfully, even if the entire show was less than perfect I was blessed to be singled out for my good performance.

"But I do have a folder of bad reviews," I finally told her, "that I bring out when I'm thinking I'm too good for my britches." It's important to listen to criticism and I do bring out those two bad reviews—yes, only two. Thank God it isn't a BIG folder!—when I need grounding. The important thing about those two reviews is that they said I wasn't working hard enough. I was coasting on the fact that I knew the audience in this particular show had come to see me. And wasn't that enough? The answer is no, it's never enough. Every performance has to be as good as you can make it. You have to do the material justice. And that's the lesson I remind myself when I see those two clippings.

So Lloyd got me into directing and I am coming full circle again, directing brand new plays. I'll talk about that later. For right now, let me say that the more arrows you have in your quiver, the more likely you are to hit that elusive target of success. When I graduated from Hunter College, I was well versed and rehearsed in all aspects of performing and I was prepared to meet the world.

THE FIRST RULE OF SHOW BUSINESS IS THERE ARE NO RULES

I think some people want to know other peoples' stories because they want to have a road map for success. Believe me, if there was such a thing as a road map for success I would be preaching it! But there isn't. Every life is full of so many marvelous variables that how can you model yours after someone else's? They may have had a stronger support system, or maybe they had to spend a lot of energy developing a support system. They may have not have had the mentors to tell them to expand their specialties. Or maybe they were showbiz royalty and there isn't any way you can duplicate that if it isn't your birthright. And why would you want to anyway? The fun of life is discovering, challenging yourself, creating your own story.

And then I heard about a movement afoot to sell the strategy of "success" or maybe it's the concept of "booking" a job.

Strategy versus Teaching

It is 5:30 AM, and my mind would not stop racing about the subject of strategy versus teaching in our business of show.

Now don't get me wrong, if your aspiration is to "work" in the business and make a decent living then maybe—and I say maybe—the strategy method is for you. But why not just choose to go to a corporate structure if you just want to work a gig and make that dollar? Corporate pays more, work is more consistent and there are better benefits for the middle level participants, and that is what you are settling for right? A middle level career? Who chooses to aspire to the middle? You may never reach the pinnacle of your dreams but my thoughts are that you must always strive for the pinnacle not midway!

This concept that there is a strategy for success that is being touted about, angers and distresses me. There should always be five year plans and goals to conquer, yes, but a step-by-step way to achieve that goal I believe is a pipe dream. Too many elements are involved for there to be a specific formula that works for everyone.

Talent levels, appearance, product demand, personal aptitude, personality, intelligence, networking and conversational skills, not to mention who you know, who you have impressed or pissed off, your support system in and out of your immediate family, spiritual commitments, education, and your social skills are just a small number of factors that will determine where you will head.

Recently someone posted on social media an advertisement presenting an idea of a series of coaching methods that will lead to breaking into a segment of the business. I believe the term was referred to as being "unstuck." Now, I agree reinvention is the name of the game in our business for everyone but especially those of us who are not considered the "commercially acceptable types," because, yes, this is a business and certain standards of employability are here to stay. Unfortunately, certain stereotypes will always be in demand and that is the business that we have bought into, but the method by which we individually achieve our personal advancement, both cannot and should not be sold like a magic elixir.

Proclaiming to dispense with spiritual connections and believing we have complete control over our destiny…well, I don't want to stand next to you in the next thunderstorm!

Spiritual guidance, I believe, is the basis for a well-rounded human being and vulnerability is the key to our reaching our audience. These two elements combined with some of the good business suggestions (and there are some good ones) make a more competent, disciplined performer, a performer I would choose when I am casting for my projects as a director or a producer.

Yes, let me get into that for a moment. Since the age of 19, I have initiated projects, directed and produced projects that have employed and paid actors, singers and musicians. It has not made me a millionaire but I think it qualifies me as a good judge for what makes an employable performer. I admit to making incorrigible, stupid, offensive mistakes with lovely actors early on, but experience is the best teacher and I stand now as an unconditional supporter of the professional performer.

I think those new to the business or those who have been in the business and plateaued or are not willing to acknowledge it is time to move to another age group and type—in other words, reinvent themselves—need to examine their current position. I say there is no quick fix, no add water and stir program. An honest look at what your responsibility is in the equation: Like, what is selling? What are audiences buying? A heavy dose of spiritual guidance and strong self -esteem and damn hard work are just the start of the elements needed to succeed. No quick scheme or scam should be chosen as a pathway to success, but a program set up by you or a trusted teacher or guidance person that focuses on your strengths first, your talent range, and then apply those strengths to the element of the business, perhaps in a new way. Teachers do this, not quick fix coaches. Teachers like the late Lloyd Richards and Frank Hatchett, the wonderful Vera Roberts, the splendid Dyane Harvey-Salaam and beautiful performers like Carmen DeLavallade dispense the love and the discipline needed for longevity in this business. Look them up and see what made them special, then study with those still alive and practicing. There are scores more of competent, guiding, sensitive teachers that are here for you. Now do your work, get off your ass and find them, and stop being scammed by imitators. There is work to be done and to be had. Go get it and stop looking for quick fixes!

Summing it up: Creativity versus just working. Why just work when you can create. We need creators in this business. Any excess other than that is expendable.

Observances

It's not old school. It's the only school.

I think that there is a misconception or a misinterpretation of the use of the phrase "old school." In my opinion, we all need to use the foundations that are dispensed in the old school methods. Learning how to sustain the voice when singing or speaking, learning how to memorize lines and accepting that becoming a performer you are a role model, will always be important. These factors don't just belong to the old school category. It is the only school. Then to younger performers: if you want to apply all of the discoveries that you have on top of these foundations, you can then go on to do anything you want.

You can go from opera to rap without taking long absences to save your voice. You can go from Shakespeare to avant-garde without dropping lines. And never mind going from theater to television to film knowing that they are three different kinds of media learned in the old school and applying them to anything. I have referenced this specifically in show business terms, but it is applicable to any business. Just take the old school lessons and apply new discoveries on top.

Advice: Distractions

I said there were no rules for succeeding in show business, but I didn't say I had no advice! I do.

One of the most important things a person has to think about when deciding to go into show business is how to deal with the many distractions that will be encountered.

Now, we all know the distractions of gratuitous use of either drugs or liquor or both. That's another chapter. No, I am talking the human distraction.

I think that when you are young, if possible you should define what your goals are and as best as you can stick to them. Relationships…family and social life are a challenge and you have to be clear how to distribute your time. Family should always be a priority and in no way am I suggesting that you neglect your familial duties. I think that you should, however, sit down and discuss your plans, passions and aspirations so everyone will understand the demands the business puts on its participants. You miss births, birthday parties, weddings, funerals. All holidays are big performance days. Just like people who work in retail, holidays are our busy days and are never spent with loved ones.

I recall my first Thanksgiving and Christmas spent away

from my nuclear family. It was strange. For Thanksgiving I was in California celebrating in 85 degree weather, eating delicious lobster, while my entire family was feasting on my mother's famous turkey, homemade stuffing, sweet potato pie, caramel cake, and all my favorites. I loved the excitement of performing and being in LA with my husband, but our families were so far away. It was weird, but we got through it.

The next Christmas I was on a Broadway Stage performing as a Christmas gift for a sold out house of theatre patrons. What a compliment! But that family traditional early Christmas morning giving of gifts would have to wait for another time.

So what I am saying is that you find a new normal. You adjust, and then when you occasionally can celebrate with the family (if you get along with them) then have fun.

Now to that person you choose as your partner. This has got to be done with great caution and with many conversations for them to try to understand your passion. I cannot emphasize enough the necessity to communicate: absolutely necessary for a healthy relationship. Children and partners: be fair to them and to yourself and plan wisely.

Life is a crap shoot. You want to give it your best shot. No do-overs, you know. Take your time and choose wisely: your career, your distractions, your partners, your time. It's your choice and yours alone.

Advice: The Scariest Part of a Young Performer's Life...the audition!

In many books performers talk of the audition process.

My opinion and school of thought: "There are no lessons for it. You just have to keep doing them until you find your zone and if that zone sells you, you got it."

I got to the point where I loved the audition as much as I loved getting and doing the job. I loved the room. I tried to do my research on the people in the room as well as our people behind the desk. I did research on the piece. Each session was a challenge…a performance…what fun!

I realize some people hate auditions and declare they are awful at them and maybe they are. If you get the hang of them, though, they are good for you. If you still think you are bad at them, then work on a solution. Showcase yourself in different ways. Write or find material that is surely you and work on it. Present yourself in the best light. That's all auditions are anyway. Enjoy the performance. After all if you don't enjoy doing this then you should be doing something else!

My Journey

And of course you can learn things from other peoples' journeys. Who did they know? How did they make those connections? Because more than anything, show business is a people business. You can't make those same connections, but you can learn the lesson that connections—backed up with rigorous preparation, a strong support system, and burning desire of course—are everything.

Here is my story.

The Beginning

Where would any of us be without the influences of our

formative years? My parents Fred and Maggie Godfrey were my role models for hard work, honor, self-confidence, vision, spiritual and intellectual guidance and street smarts to name a few of the qualities they passed on to me.

But I was out there in the world too and learning things not necessarily taught by my parents or found in books.

I had graduated from the private school I had attended since elementary school, The Modern School, headed by Mildred L. Johnson (niece of James Weldon Johnson, author of the Black National Anthem *Lift Every Voice And Sing*) assisted by Eva DesVerney and Mildred's mother Mrs. N.E. Johnson.

Here I had learned French and English language elocution and articulation from the formidable Mrs. Eleanora B. Sellers, a woman whose insistence on perfection stays with me to this day. Poise, grace and some musical understanding were handed to students by Mildred herself. This was just prior to my Carnegie Hall training with Dr. Chauncey Northern, Sr.

The small graduating class of thirteen gave me pause and reason to want to be challenged by a more public environment. Don't get me wrong, I loved the intimacy that the private school provided but I longed to be in front of a larger audience, and that is what I found.

Then the beautiful George Washington High School sat atop a hill on a grassy knoll in Washington Heights in Manhattan—population 5,000 students. Jo-Ann, who was older, was a student at George Washington High School, and upon visiting her there, I fell in love with the school and its campus. It was a very competitive environment and my goal was to conquer it and that I did. First as a freshman I became Student Government Representative of my freshman and sophomore class, as a sophomore/junior I was elected Manhattan Council President and then as junior/senior the first and only female President of the Student Body in the history of the school. George Washington High School alum includes former Chairman of the Federal Reserve Alan Greenspan, although years before me, of course.

I sang my first solo there and thrilled the school with my voice. They were used to sopranos and for the first time they heard a small girl with a deep, rich, and loud baritone-to-soprano range voice. I was encouraged to sing and accompanied by then-senior Kenneth Hanson. Kenneth went on to stage manage shows like *The Wiz* and *Jelly's Last Jam* and is a Broadway staple. Thank you Kenny for all your help back then.

I was full of indecision in those days on whether to follow the advice of the academic experts and go to a popular private institutions or to follow my heart and passion. As usual I followed my heart. Though my decisions are not always the most popular choice with my supporters, I always need to follow my heart and passion.

This experience instilled leadership qualities that stay with me each time I pick up a script to direct or stand alone on a stage and tell stories through dialogue or song.

It was a combination of the performances festivals held twice a year, Spring and Christmas at The Modern School, and the appearances daily before a student body of thousands that set me on my way from politics to performance. All who knew me back then surely thought I would emerge as the next *Perry Mason*…oh well… you better believe I can play the hell out of Perry if I had to.

What I did not mention before was that because I was President of the School I was selected by Exxon as a student intern for the summer after graduation with about eight other students as I remember. As I recall, I was the only student retained and I spent every summer and vacation as a Student Executive of the Marine Sales Department of Exxon until my college graduation when I decided not to pursue a career in oil but to go into performance.

Climbing to Broadway One step at a Time— College

Graduating from George Washington High School with honors it was not hard to figure college was the next step. My vocal teacher, Dr. Northern, was an alumnus of Hampton Institute (or University as it was called when I attended) and thought it a good idea for me to attend to continue the tradition as he became family to me.

Even to take classes in the music department, an audition was required. As memory serves, I auditioned with the Tosca aria *Vissi D'Arte* and I was admitted to the department.

Two very important things happened. Again the lesson—know yourself.

I have a vocal range that is wide and most vocal teachers favor the higher more traditional portion of my voice. The then-head of the voice department at Hampton thought he would take my dramatic soprano voice and make it into a first soprano. About three weeks into vocal exercises, exercises that I thought were totally inappropriate, I went home to let Dr. Northern hear my voice. He was appalled. He ordered me into vocal silence for six weeks and demanded that I immediately change my focus to theatre. What good fortune.

I should say my voice recovered completely but what was to happen next was a pure blessing. Not luck, a blessing!

I dropped voice and theory, which I was not doing well in, silently finished the semester and that made it possible to remain on the Dean's List.

I changed my academic focus so the the next semester brought me a Speech class and the wonderful theatre pioneer Marjorie Moon who was teaching that course at the time. She suggested, as I mentioned earlier, that I audition for Sonia Sanchez's Sister Sonji . I caught the bug and the rest is history. I transferred to Hunter College, studied in New York City with Dr. Northern at Carnegie Hall and Lloyd Richards at Hunter College and the performer Lynnie Godfrey was born!

What did I learn? Well, that when you follow your dreams and have great guidance, things fall into place. God and fate take over. I was meant to study with Dr. Northern, who knew my voice, and to discover and learn from the brilliance of Lloyd Richards at Hunter College who knew everything I needed to know about theatre!

Within three years after meeting Lloyd and consistently studying with Dr. Northern, I was on the Broadway stage in *EUBIE!* But first...

One Thing Leads to Another

My first audition was before I even graduated from college. I believed I had something special and I couldn't wait to share it with the world. At Hunter at that time, you didn't have to take exams if you were pulling an A average and I was, so there I was, a senior with some time on my hands. Craig Belknap (Allen), my Acting 101 teacher asked me to audition for an off-Broadway show he was directing. I got the part, but my mentors, Vera Roberts and Lloyd Richards, said absolutely not! Not even as an understudy!

What they understood was that I still had a great deal to learn.

Lloyd helped me prepare for my career. He helped me prepare for auditions which is very important—a lot of people don't know how to. To me, an audition is like a performance. You have to present yourself in just the same way. Having Vera and Lloyd as mentors to guide and advise me helped me make the right decisions. To have taken this role, I would have had to drop out of school and as it turns out, the play closed before it opened.

Before graduation, I auditioned for and got my first job. It was for the play *Mama Liberty*. The theatre was Theater for the New City. A fellow actor in the production, Alvin Alexis, recently reminded me that Tim Robbins was also in that play—I played Mama Liberty—but I hope I can be forgiven for not remembering him, because although Tim was very distinctive looking—he is 6'4"—he was wearing a mask of, I think, Dean Haldeman! Almost everyone wore a mask. I didn't, though. I played Mama Liberty—who was symbolic of the Statue of Liberty. It was a very political play.

Soon after that same summer I got another call from Craig Belknap. This time he wanted me to audition for the part of a dark angel, Elaine, in Christopher Durang's long one-act play, *The Nature and Purpose of the Universe*, to be presented at the Direct Theatre in New York City. The play simulated a lot of violence—my character was always beating up on someone—but the violence was mitigated by the fact that the play was presented as if it were a radio play. The actors stayed mainly in place in front of microphones and the violence was presented in off-scene sound effects.

This was a comedic/dramatic play—although when they found out I could sing, they put a song in it for me—so when I saw the call to audition for *Ragtime Blues*, the story of Scott Joplin, I was eager to audition. This was for AMAS Repertory Theatre (they were responsible for initiating the wonderful hit *Bubblin' Brown Sugar*). The Artistic Director was Rosetta Lenoir. As I mentioned earlier, I got the part of Scott's first wife, Belle, who was just evil! At one point she burned all of his music and then, when she was asked what she did with Scott's music said, "Sent it up the chimney to Santa Claus!" To this day, people who saw me in that production still greet me with that line. What fun it was.

Right after that I was in *Voices Inc.*. This is where I met theatre veteran Sheila Kay Davis. We did the history of the African race in America in the first act from slavery to freedom was done A cappella and then the second act had music. We toured regionally. While I was performing in this I saw an ad in Backstage or Show Business for auditions for a musical in Amsterdam. I thought, of course, Amsterdam, New York, but it was Amsterdam, Holland!

I set up the audition which was in Mildred Kayden's (who wrote the music and lyrics) very stylish apartment on the East Side of Manhattan. I still remember the beautiful grand piano in her living room. Anyway, they were looking for someone to play both Josephine Baker and Marlene Dietrich and as I was waiting in the foyer with the other wannabees, I couldn't help but notice I was the only Black woman auditioning. But that didn't bother me. That never bothered me. And when I walked into the audition space, Mildred looked up at me and said simply, "Well, there you are" and I was hired.

Amsterdam

Doing the character of Josephine Baker/Marlene

34

Dietrich was absolutely challenging and fantastic.

The production company flew all seven of the cast to Amsterdam. It was the first time I was out of the country and really nothing can prepare you for that. Everything was different. The food was wonderful: almond paste, pound cake, gyros, and mayonnaise on French fries. What a wonderful combination that is! I had to put the brakes on that, though, because I had to be in top shape for my role in *AbsurDities*, which was billed as the funniest vaudeville show ever and my costume was very little most of the time. My face was used as the basis for the drawing on the poster. But there was the food problem. Everything was delicious and I could easily go to the market—with my fishnet bag of course!—and buy the most wonderful things to eat.

The theater where we performed was the Theater Frascatti which had a café attached. The chef there, a brilliantly handsome man—all Dutch men are handsome, I think—asked me how I liked the food and I had to admit it was a bit rich for me. He said, "I have just the thing for you!" and he prepared the most delicious omelet for me which turns out to be the best food for performing. It gives you energy but doesn't bog you down. To this day, I eat an omelet every day when I am performing.

Europe was nothing like I expected. The taxis were Mercedes Benz for one thing. I had thought all Europeans got along, but I soon found out the Dutch disliked the Germans who disliked the English who disliked everyone. I learned to stay out of that. The most fabulous memory I have is walking down one of the main streets headed for the theatre and having a tour bus stop alongside of me. The windows were open and all the tourists were snapping pictures....of me! I do have a dramatic style of dressing—of course I do!—but it was funny to be taken as a native of

Amsterdam when I was as much of a tourist as they were.

But I was lonely. I had left my then-fiancé in New York (this relationship ended shortly after I returned to New York City) and I was determined to be an honorable woman—although I was asked out all the time by stage door Johnnies who sent their wives home right after the show. The rest of the cast was paired off, so I was really alone. There were no cell phones or internet then, remember, and communication was not as easy as it is now. The show was booked from July to September and we were extended—it was a great hit!—and by the time the show finally closed in early winter, I was more than ready to come home.

92d St. Y or Name Dropping At Its Best

It is 2015 and I am speaking with my new friend Ms. Melba Tolliver, the first Black Anchor of Network Television. She mentions that she and a friend were attending a Conversation at 92nd Street Y with Brian Grazer and Malcom Gladwell. Wonderful memories of working there come back to me.

It was a bit after my Broadway stint with *EUBIE!* and I was honored to be asked to participate in a Music Series headed by the late wonderful Maurice Levine.

I had been asked to work with Burton Lane (known as the man who discovered Judy Garland) composer of great works like the Broadway production of *Finian's Rainbow* and the wonderful ballad *On a Clear Day*, which I love singing. For the Music Series, I sang *Necessity* from *Finian's* and worked with the wonderful late and marvelously talented Larry Kert (the original Tony in the original Broadway version of *West Side Story*). Larry, what a dream to work with! I would go on to work with him in another production, *Knickerbocker Follies,* in New York where he performed his wonderful interpretation of Al Jolson. What a dream.

Burton would invite Larry and me to his East Hampton home. We were to perform in the Hamptons in a show Burton put together featuring Larry and myself. Larry Kert, my husband Carl and I became good friends. Larry once went on television and quoted Carl on something. It started like this, "Lynnie Godfrey's husband Carl Lee says…" I don't remember what he went on to say but it tickled us pink to be his friend. Working with Larry and Burton was so wonderful. I had no idea how wonderful until I look back on it. Learning from giants in my field. What an education.

Other shows at the 92nd Street had me performing songs from Burton Lane, Livingston and Evans (they wrote the theme to TVs *Bonanza* and the title song for the movie *Tammy* which the fabulous Debbie Reynolds recorded). I remember them telling me how when she sang it for the first time it was almost exactly what we hear on the recording. Such generous gentlemen! I remember keeping in contact with them years later when I was working in Los Angeles. Sammy Cahn the great composer hosted one show I participated in and the phenomenal Betty Hutton was a guest on another show. We shared a dressing room for the performance and I recall how quiet and gracious she was. It was later in life for her and she was so humble and lovely. She didn't talk much but was so kind.

What great lessons of professionalism, humility, grace and poise I learned as I watched these great performers do their thing. As I look back on the experiences I am truly honored and amazed I got to be a participant in these events. Thanks Maurice Levine, Burton Lane and 92nd Street Y for the opportunities.

My First Sitcom Job

After *EUBIE!*, regional theater, and the 92d St. Y, I had gone to Los Angeles on a bet with my husband. He thought I could work there. We had seen so many of my talented Broadway friends segue their way to film and television work and his ambitious reasoning was that I could also.

I had been told by a friend's manager that I was and would always be a character performer—not an actress (even though I had studied acting with the best teacher in the business. I just had not told him). He felt I needed to stick to the broad performances of the theatre where they loved my creative choices.

However, this time I was bored with the limited choices that the industry had decided I could do. I also realized I had done nothing to cause the industry executives to change their mind. Important lesson: take responsibility for your own position in the industry. Empower yourself with changing your position. Reinvention is a powerful word in the right hands.

The bet with my husband was that I stay in Los Angeles for three months and if nothing happened I could return home. I went to stay three months and stayed ten years. He was right.

Some of the details of my first six weeks are boring and mundane: adjustment, homesickness, self-transformation—all interesting in their own way—but when I owned the idea that it was an opportunity to develop my talents on a different plane and receive wider recognition I was off to the races.

After getting an agent in LA through the New York

agent I was working with at the time, I waited for six weeks before my first call, but I was ready when it came. I had worked on transforming the strong make-up of the Broadway stage to the softness of the on camera look—a small role in a New York based movie the year before I left for Los Angeles helped me know I needed the make-up and acting transitions.

I got the first call, a commercial. Booked it! Then a second call, a play. Booked it! The wonderful play *No Place to Be Somebody* by the brilliant Charles Gordone at the Matrix Theatre at Melrose Avenue in LA. I received the NAACP and Dramalogue awards for Best Supporting Actress (for the role of Cora Mae Beasley in *No Place to Be Somebody* originally created by the formidable Mary Alice, with whom I would go on to appear in an episode of LA Law.) Then a third call, a Saturday morning television program called *The New Monkees* in a recurring role of Helen the Computer. Booked it! How grand! I could work in LA and get paid, paid a lot!

Small dramatic roles (on wonderful programs like *Frank's Place*) followed. What a great experience playing the daughter to the fabulous Beah Richards and watching other stars glide so easily through the tasks of film and television. What a blessing and what lessons. Lessons that can and will never be learned in any classroom. Which is why I say that "practical experience" is best for a performer in training unless a teacher can provide you with studio or film experience.

Finally, a call came for an audition for a situation comedy. I had been in Los Angeles all of seven months when it came. I had booked enough so the casting agents of the time were comfortable with bringing me in. I was recommended to come in and do a role about a *femme fatale* at a school reunion on the then quite popular NBC series,

Amen. The wonderful Rueben Cannon was casting, such a nice man to me, and …Booked it! The details I share at my Master Classes and lectures, you have to sit in sometime, but it was a blast audition and most importantly in this audition was a veteran writer named Art Julian. It was Art who then decided to make the *femme fatale* Jackie Dunn the best friend of Thelma Frye the lead (played by the fabulous and lovely Anna Maria Horsford) and a lifelong TV and real life friendship was born.

Before I go on to talk about the lovely experience I had on the set I would like to salute Ms. Anna Maria Horsford. I had not done any situation comedies until *Amen* and what a lovely beginning. Ms. Horsford set the example of the hostess/star of a program that inspired me then and continues to inspire me to be the best example of a leader on any set…television, film or theatre. She was and still is gracious, welcoming, genuinely friendly. It was the example I followed when allowed to lead my own cast on *704 Hauser.*

I did those episodes with Anna, theatre legend Barbara Montgomery and talented Roz Ryan. And what fun they were! I went on to do more than 30 guest roles and I can clearly say that no other set made me feel as welcome as *Amen.* I had more fun and enjoyed relationships with these ladies more than any others I would go on to work with in Los Angeles.

So why this story? First, never believe anyone's opinion about your own limitations whether it is professionally doing someone's make-up, teaching, typing speeds or performing. Had I listened to the experts, I would not have ventured out. I would not have not shown the self-confidence to land the work.

Self-confidence. You know your strengths and weaknesses. You test them and can blame no one when you do nothing.

Another thing: Faith in God to guide you, not expecting God do all the work while you idly wait for something to happen. God helps those who help themselves so get off you *ss and do something.

Also: when the call comes be ready. If there is time between jobs work on yourself, get a job and hone your office skills, waiting skills, paralegal skills, it might come in handy for a role. Don't be a lazy actor, work your muscles, exercise your skills, stretch, vocalize whether you're singing/performing that day or not, and know the business end of the business.

Back to the Boards

CBS didn't renew *704 Hauser.* The passing of my parents, specifically my father before the show started its run and my mother a year after the show ended, affected my life and career decisions. I decided that then was time for me to come back East.

But as luck—*opportunity + preparedness = luck!*—would have it, another door opened for me.

The Snow Queen

Patricia Snyder, Executive Artistic Director of the NYSTI (New York State Theater Institute), acquired the rights to *The Snow Queen* (book and lyrics by Adrian Mitchell, Music by Richard Peaslee) and Patricia Birch, the director, immediately thought to cast me. She knew my work from the Knickerbocker Rock Festival where I performed with Jack Gilford—well-known for his role as Crackerjack in commercials—and Orson Bean. Snow

Queen is a timeless play based on the classic by Hans Christian Anderson and I was eager to do the role because although the popular perception is that the Snow Queen is evil, I don't see her that way. She's just a poor, lost soul. I believed in her and as an actress, it's important to like your character even if no one else does. If you take the audience with you—if you believe—everyone else will too.

There is also the popular perception that the Snow Queen could not ever possibly be Black and I enjoy taking on roles that are not traditionally earmarked as such.

Plus, it was the first major role I played after both my parents passed away.

The play opened in 1996 in NY to great reviews such as these:

"Lynnie Godfrey is a force of nature as the Snow Queen, swooping in all fingernails, flowing cape and icicle tiara. Her speaking voice sends all the appropriate shivers, and her singing voice is as seductive as her suggestions. She inhabits the Snow Queen so fully that when she threatens Kai with a third and final icy kiss of death, you're actually jealous of him."—Michael Eck, *The Times Union*, December 11, 1996.

"As the Snow Queen, Lynnie Godfrey is excellent. She projects a coldness to match her title, yet she is provocative without being sensual, a delicacy that is very important to a show geared to young audiences. (she) is critical to the show's success."—*The Record* by Bob Goepfert December 13, 1996

Immediately the talk was that we had to take the show to London.

Now that isn't the way things are usually done. Usually

London brings shows to us, not the other way around. And we had another obstacle: we were bringing our leading lady: me. But Adrian Mitchell was adamant, "Lynnie is our queen" and that was that. I was not happy about being alone in London for a run, especially as my parents were no longer with me, but I thought perhaps it would be good to involve myself in work.

Sadly, Carl's brother, Albert, passed away and then Carl got the word that he was being transferred to London on a temporary special assignment. We went right from the funeral to the airport and flew to London. It was before 9/11 so no one was checking anything in the airports and I flew right through. Otherwise, I'm sure I would have set off every alarm with my jewelry and occupied all the security personnel with my bags of clothing and accessories! I've learned and travel differently today.

Anyway, it was like a dream flying away with Carl and leaving all that sadness behind.

We got a flat in London and I learned how to take the underground, going to Victoria Station and changing to go to Piccadilly and walk to South Kensington where the theater was. Then at night after the show—and after I stopped at Pret-A-Manger where I ordered egg salad and guacamole to go—I took the train back to Hoxton where we lived.

I learned to love international food—and Pret-a-Manger is French—because while I adore the British people, I am not too keen on British cooking.

I shopped all the time. The vendors in Convent Garden knew me and saved all the best handbags to show me. It was a wonderful experience. I was such a frequent visitor at Harrods that one of the salespersons there subtly suggested I should just get a store credit card. He was right!

Carl came and brought all the Exxon executives with

him. They would come back to the show on Saturday with their children. Fritz Klausner, who I knew from high school days interning in Marine Sales at Exxon, came. It was thrilling. The show sold out all the time.

And we got great reviews:

"Lynnie Godfrey is a fantastically diabolic Snow Queen with a voice both spine-chilling and soul-soothing."
Unicorn theater: Review in *Stage:* John Thaxter: Feb. 3, 1998
"Lynnie Godfrey's Ice Queen, her beauty and expressive gestures recalling Diana Ross, has an extraordinary range over two octaves in thrilling key renderings of *Devil Mirror* and *Kiss of the Snow Queen."*—Ann Sinnott, *West End Extra* January 30, 1998

For me, personally, it was a healing experience from the loss of my parents. We took the Bullet Train to Paris all the time and fell in love with Europe. In fact, from 2002 to 2006 Carl and I went to Europe every year.

The show came back to the states in the Prince Theater in Philadelphia. The musical director was Charles Prince, Hal Prince's son. He was allergic to my dog (Moo Moo, a long-haired dachshund) so I didn't see too much of him because my dog was always with me, and then I just stopped bringing my dog to the theater.

Coming back to Philadelphia had brought back great memories. It was where *EUBIE!* debuted (before our B'way run) at the Walnut Street Theatre and like I mentioned earlier in this guide…broke all summer house records at that point. It was also where I met my husband. So I was anxiously looking forward to this return.

Much care had been taken to put on the production of *Snow Queen* at the Prince Theater and in this production a ramp was built to dramatize my entrance.

What I didn't realize, however, is that the ramp at the theater where I made my entrance was dangerous too. The costume designer put me in a very tight skirt and the highest heels you can imagine. They take a certain finesse to walk in under the best conditions, but coming down a wooden ramp at a forty-five degree angle in this get-up was downright hazardous. The set designer helped me out by calling for a sticky substance—which the stage manager had to reapply every night—to be painted on the ramp so I had something to hold on to which helped somewhat.

Until one night the stage manager forgot.

I was making my entrance and my right foot was searching for the stickiness and not finding it. I slid and tried to balance myself with my left foot, but that didn't find the expected patch of stickiness either. I slid, landed on my rump and slid all the way down to the stage to a standing ovation.

"Now wait!" I said, after the applause settled down. "Conductor, please take it from the top." I climbed the stairs to the top of the ramp and this time held on to the railing as I made my way down the ramp. I would not let the lack of sticky paint ruin my entrance! I received another ovation!

Lesson learned: Never be defeated. Try again!

The funny thing is, though, after that night—and after the stage hands religiously painted the ramp for me—I didn't fall and audience members would come up to me afterwards wondering what happened to my dramatic entrance. The audience thought that the fall was part of the show!

Cinderella

In 2001 I traveled to upstate New York playing the stepmother in *Cinderella*. As I said, I am really good at playing evil because I am good at making the audience understand what makes the character that way. One night, during the New York City run, Patricia Neal came to the performance. I was not the lead, so my dressing room was upstairs and after the performance I heard Ms. Neal's distinctive voice booming out, "Where is she? I want to meet her!" and when they led her to the dressing room of the actress portraying Cinderella, Ms. Neal said, "No, not her! I want to meet the woman who played the stepmother!" I was summoned and I immediately flew down the three fights of steps from my dressing room to meet that wonderful legend and we had a lovely chat. She is a wonderful woman and a wonderful actress and her praise meant a lot to me.

Gem of the Ocean

While I enjoyed breaking through color barriers and playing roles not necessarily written for Black women, I was overjoyed when I read for August Wilson's *Gem of the Ocean* (Arena Stage, Washington DC., Molly Smith, Artistic Director) for the role of Aunt Ester, a woman who is 285 years old—older than slavery the critics said. Paulette Randell was the director. It was challenging because Aunt Ester was a woman I knew, my grandmother. It was as if August Wilson had written my grandmother! I was taking on the role the wonderful actress Phylicia Rashad had done on Broadway and taking on the role always has pitfalls. You can't be another actress, even if you wanted to, because the role sort of comes in and mixes with your own personality. So I couldn't be Phylicia Rashad being Aunt Ester. I decided to go to the source. Now, all the women in my family are long-lived. My grandmother died at 94, her mother died at 112, and my grandmother's first cousin, "Cousin Mattie" as we called her lived to be 105 so I know about longevity. I know about the wisdom that comes with age. The patience. And the humor. That was what I drew on, my grandmother's humor.

My father and grandmother displayed their love of humor in their relationship and we all saw it. We laughed at times at various stories and at each other. It was that humor I drew for MY Aunt Ester, a very different choice: she was a combination of my nana and Cousin Mattie. They had seen it all.

My grandmother was a laundress. She could starch and iron clothes like nobody else on the planet. And she took real pride in what she did, which was do the laundry for all the rich white folks in her town since she was a young woman. I remember sitting on the porch with her when I was about 12 years old and this car comes down the street and my Nana says, "Here they are, bringing their nasty clothes." Then, "You know her husband is cheating on her. She's the only one who doesn't know." "How do you know that, Nana," I asked her, and she said, "I see the lipstick on his collar. And it isn't his wife's shade."

Nana and Cousin Mattie lived together. They had seen it all. And they knew all about the two faces Black people have to wear: one for themselves and one for their clients.

Ladies of Song

In 2002, the NYSTI came to me and said, "We owe you one, we owe you a product."

47

Ball of Fire, *Mildred Pearce* and a few others were suggestions of pieces that I might try out or commission, suggested by me and the theatre.

When you have a green field like that, it's hard to come up with something, but Carl Lee came to the rescue. He had a concept for a show that would illustrate the influences that three giant women had on my career: Ethel Waters, Ella Fitzgerald and Sarah Vaughn. Not to impersonate them, but to pay tribute to them. What's the use of impersonation? There are records available for that. I wanted to show the talent and the hunger these women had that enabled them to become stars. As well as all the sacrifices they had to make. I wanted to sing their music, but infuse it with my own soul. That was the basis of *Ladies of Song.*

I sang songs that were representative of them, told something of their lives and their unique struggles. My own struggles in the business certainly contributed to the empathy I feel for these women. Listen, fame can be addictive and a lot of people let being an entertainer dominate their life. It can become your family, your husband, your lover, your everything. Luckily, I always had a life off the stage, but I certainly know how difficult it is to create a life for yourself when you're not working.

In the last part of the show, I feature work that I put my own stamp on. From the show, *EUBIE!* I sit on the piano and sing Blake and Sissle's *Daddy Won't You Please Come Home?*

Me too. I was glad to be home.

ICONS

My loving parents Maggie Mae Wood Godfrey
and Fred "Buster" Godfrey in 1945

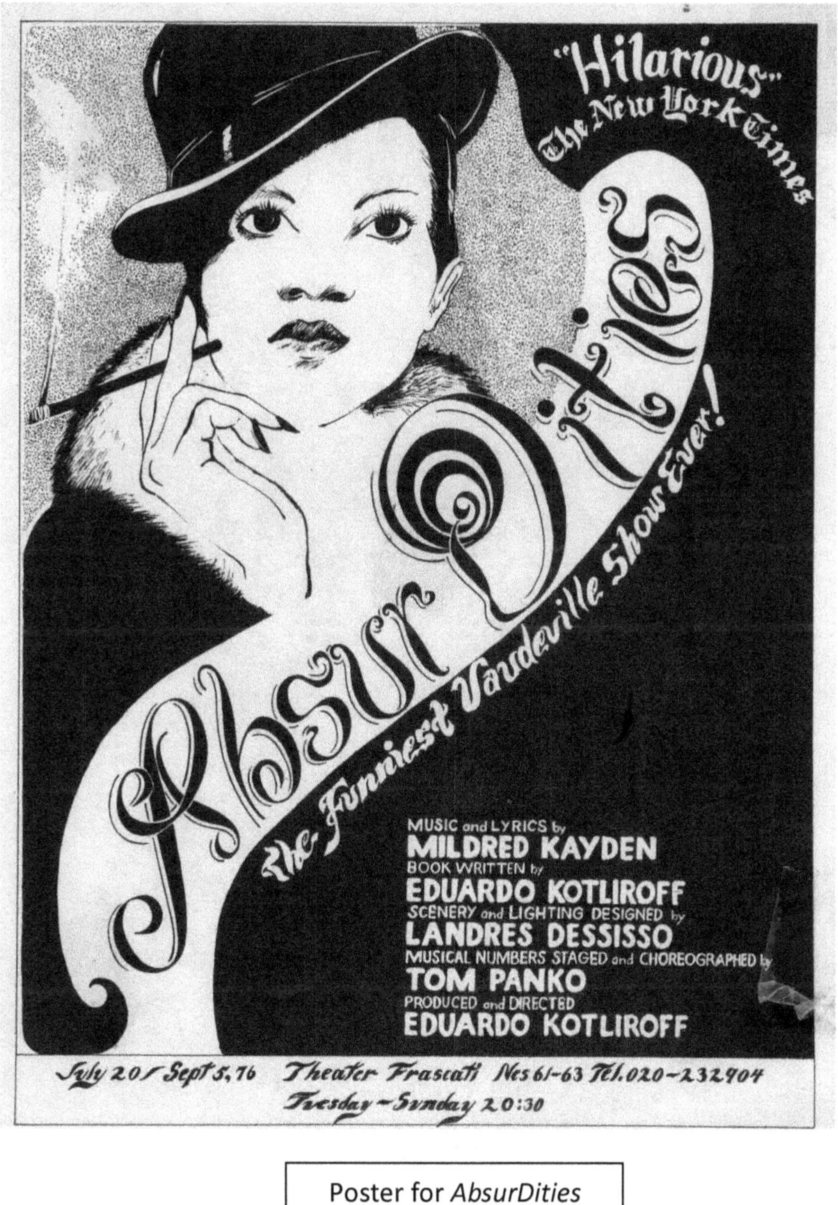

Poster for *AbsurDities*

Sweetwaters nightclub shot

Photo: Marty Wohl

Black is beautiful

Photo: Roy Blakey

Hear SONGS FROM SISSLE & BLAKE'S 1921 Hit Musical

WITH
DABRIAH CHAPMAN
LYNNIE GODFREY
ROGER LAWSON
VERNON SPENCER

CHOREOGRAPHED BY DANA MANNO
MUSICAL DIRECTION BY ADA JANIK
SET AND COSTUME DESIGN BY LEE MAYMAN
LIGHTING DESIGN BY BOYD MASTEN
PRODUCTION STAGE MANAGER ABIGAIL HARPER

Shuffle Along

All performances at 8p.m.
Feb. 2,3,5 no performance Feb.4
Feb. 9,10,11,12
Feb. 15,16,17,18,19
SOLD OUT

DIRECTED BY JULIANNE BOYD

AT THEATRE OFF PARK
28 E 35 ST
Res. 683-4991 Donations $3.00/TDF
an equity approved showcase

New York Showcase that led to the Broadway Musical *EUBIE!!!*

Playbill for *EUBIE!* Walnut St. Theatre in Philadelphia

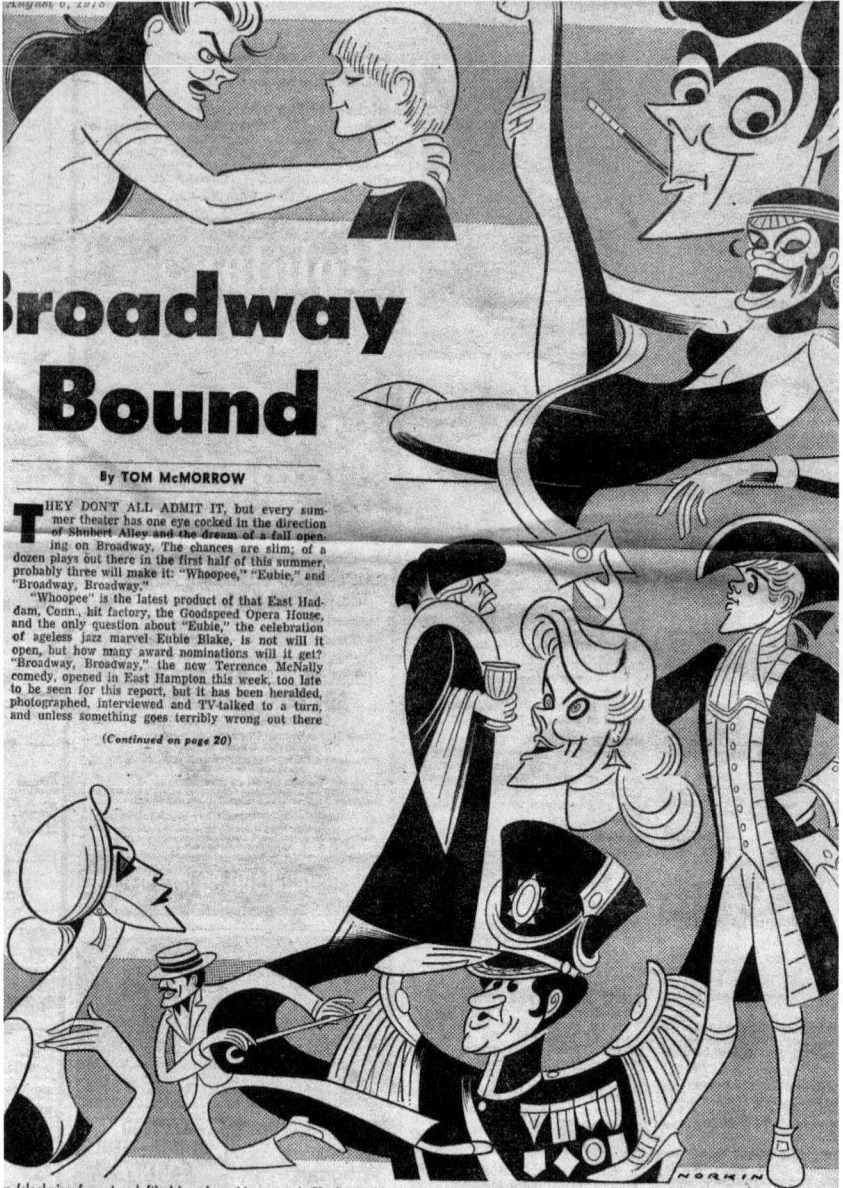

Broadway
Bound

By TOM McMORROW

THEY DON'T ALL ADMIT IT, but every summer theater has one eye cocked in the direction of Shubert Alley and the dream of a fall opening on Broadway. The chances are slim; of a dozen plays out there in the first half of this summer, probably three will make it: "Whoopee," "Eubie," and "Broadway, Broadway."

"Whoopee" is the latest product of that East Haddam, Conn. hit factory, the Goodspeed Opera House, and the only question about "Eubie," the celebration of ageless jazz marvel Eubie Blake, is not will it open, but how many award nominations will it get? "Broadway, Broadway," the new Terrence McNally comedy, opened in East Hampton this week, too late to be seen for this report, but it has been heralded, photographed, interviewed and TV-talked to a turn, and unless something goes terribly wrong out there

(Continued on page 20)

s (clockwise from top left): Mary-Joan Negro and Charlie Fields in "Put Them All Together"; Charles Repole in "Whoopee"; Lynnie Godfre
Redgrave in "Twelfth Night";

Pre-Broadway publicity for *EUBIE!*   Sam Norkin drawing

Broadway Playbill for EUBIE!
Opening night September 20, 1978

"Lynnie Godfrey has a voice that can crush diamonds: she sings *Daddy* on top of a piano accompanied by the single most eloquent leg in Western Civilization." Jack Kroll in *Newsweek* October 2, 1978, review of *EUBIE!*

Photo: Bert Andrews

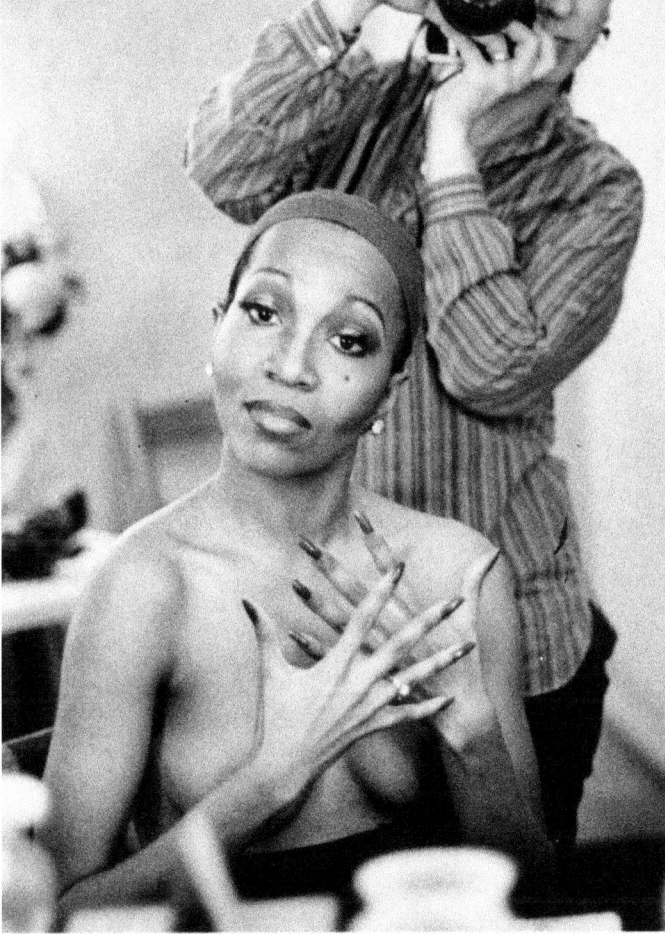

Backstage preparing for *EUBIE!* Performance
Photo: Rivka Shifman

String Bean Lynnie as Ethel Waters, one of
my favorite role models

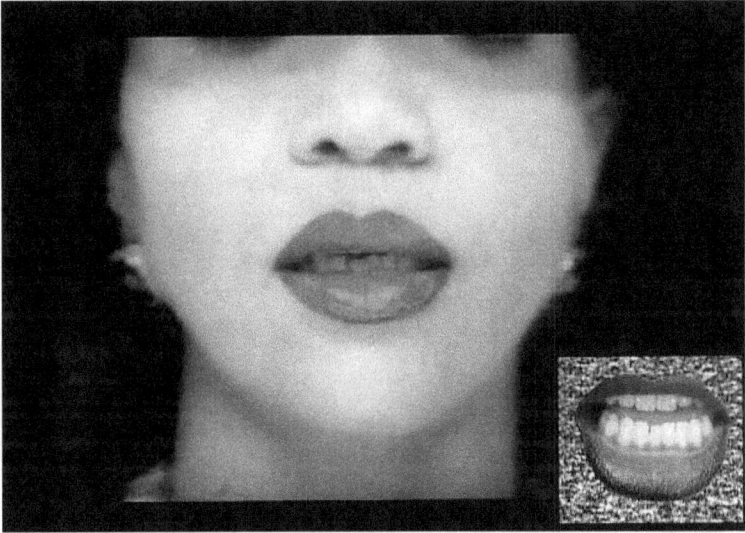

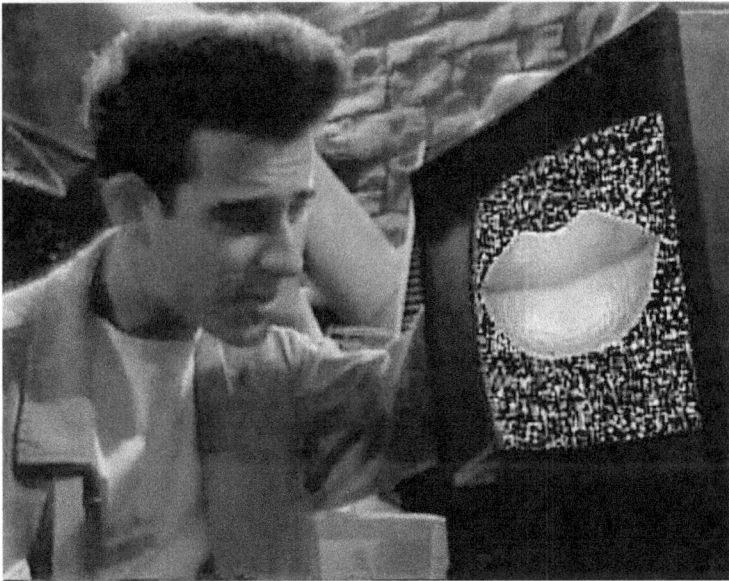

Helen the Computer in *The New Monkees*.
What great fun!

Portraying Cora Mae Beasley in this Pulitzer Prize winning
play was absolutely marvelous. I received the NAACP and
Dramalogue awards for Best Supporting Actress.

Cast of *704 Hauser*, Norman Lear CBS Series. Bottom left: John Amos, right: me. Top left: Maura Tierney, right: T. E.Russell

The Snow Queen, New York. One of the best roles ever!
With Ashton Holmes

Photo: Richard Finkelstein

NYS Theatre Institute 1997-1998 Season

THE SNOW QUEEN

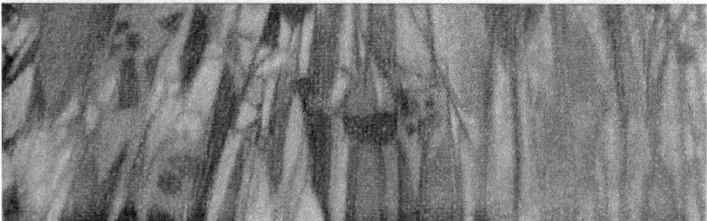

Playbill for The Snow Queen

A one-woman tribute to wonderful ladies

Divine Diva

By James Yeara

Ladies of Song: An Homage to Ethel Waters, Ella Fitzgerald, and Sarah Vaughan

BY MAX SMARR, BASED ON A CONCEPT BY CARL E. LEE, DIRECTED BY ROBERT BENNETT STEINMAN

NEW YORK STATE THEATRE INSTITUTE, SCHACHT FINE ARTS CENTER, THROUGH FEB. 18.

WITH GORGEOUS COSTUMES BY Brent Griffin fill

sing them.

Waters—"Sweet Mama Stringbean," as Godfrey-as-Waters tells us—is created as a beautiful angry woman. Godfrey captures Waters' anger at her upbringing, her poverty, her treatment at the hands of men. Godfrey sings the Arlen-and-Koehler standard created for Waters, "Stormy Weather," in a breathy chest voice that comm____rs' experience as interpreted

Times Union

ENCORE

'Ladies' a sensuous portrait of 3 divas

STAGE REVIEW

By MICHAEL ECK
Special to the Times Union

TROY — "Je'

ARTS & ENTERTAINMENT

'Ladies of Song' is a glorious show

MONDAY, FEBRUARY 4, 2008
THE DAILY GAZETTE

REVIEW

By PAUL LAMAR
For The Daily Gazette

Critiques of *Ladies of Song*

Jazz Upstairs

OBSTACLE IS JUST ANOTHER WORD FOR OPPORTUNITY

Growth versus Change

With the onslaught of all these personal tragedies and the change in the business it was time to re-assess my life and career. The business is always evolving and the programs I enjoyed so much were fading out and a new breed of television was being developed. I believe in growth in life and business, however I think we have to know the difference between change and growth.

I think the terms "growth" and "change" are not interchangeable. So many times when people want to indicate that there will be a difference in their behavior they think that either term will apply. I disagree. I think one can evolve in one's personal development and that shows growth. Change encompasses several elements: your tastes start to vary; your preference in people undergoes a renewal; your life path, the way you envision your future takes on a new shape.

Home isn't Always Where You Hang Your Hat

I'd like to think that with my skills I could live anywhere and be happy, that even if I didn't like a place, per se, I could find some way to turn the physical location to my advantage. But I have found, and you will too, that there are places where you can live successfully and places where you cannot. Being aware of that will help you make a key decision and that is when it's time to leave.

Twice I have tried a Southern state as a place to settle. Both times in Virginia. In both instances I found the state beautiful and the people gracious. What I also found is that in both instances the places were transient: a campus for students and their four to five years, or a beautiful bedroom community built for imported executives.

Living in Virginia was amicable, but I found that like other places that attract executives and students—New York, Los Angeles, Houston, for example—it didn't have the warmth of a place where people come because they want to be there, not because they have to be there to achieve something. It can be cold, yes, but you have to find your way as well as friendships and meaningful relationships.

I love New York because I was born and raised there. My high school and college friends all still come to see me entertain. I have a history there. My family lived and passed away there and in New Jersey. My ties run deep and there is no one who lives there that is more of a New Yorker than I am. But imagine coming to New York City at the age of nineteen or twenty-one. Your goal is success as it would be in LA or Houston, etc. No time for relationships that do not further your career. I do understand that time is of the essence and there is a certain time in your life where you have to make things happen. But if you have already made those things happen in your own life and are looking for lasting friendships, you might want to reconsider settling in success driven communities.

It took a little while to realize it wasn't me. But I did catch on! You have to choose a place to live whose pace and priorities coincide with where you are in life. I now reside where people and my many new friends have chosen to be. I live where people are already successful and enjoy the relationships they have by choice.

Time to For a Change

Things were changing in the business and surely my life had changed and decisions had to be made.

I was not right or comfortable with some of the roles offered and I needed to reinvent once again the performer called LYNNIE GODFREY.

Time for a radical change. I thought at first that the corporate move to Virginia was just what I needed. But as I've known since I was young, I am a Northeastern girl and my desire for that region made my eleven year stay in Virginia not as productive as I would have liked. Oh, performances at the Kennedy Center and the famed Arena Stage and meeting lovely performers there made it fun at times, but I knew I had to return to my roots.

After about ten years, my husband, Carl, and I started a quiet search for change in my life and career.

Living Here in the Lehigh Valley

I am now a resident of the Lehigh Valley. How did that happen? Why did you pick the Lehigh Valley? I am asked so often. It is a condescending question, I think. But for one thing, the Lehigh Valley is beautiful and convenient to another place I call home, New York City.

In our Lehigh Valley community, it is a fertile place for performing and creativity. It is the perfect place for me.

The opportunities are unique and endless.

It brings peace whenever I arrive on Highway 78. My breathing slows down and the corners of my mouth start to make a smile. It is just a wonderful place to live. My neighbors are lovely, those that I know, and they let me be me.

A great place to live.

From The Darkness To The Cabaret Stage

There is a gap I need to fill in. For almost five to seven years I did not sing a note on the stage. There was no vocal issue, there was a creative issue. I have sung all the songs given to me by people I thought knew what I could do. I was wrong (as the lyric in *Lush Life* says) Ah yes, I was wrong. No one knew me that well except my vocal teacher Chauncey Northern Sr. and he passed away in 1992.

I have sung it all: "money" note songs (and if you are in the business and don't know what that is, shame on you), songs that show off your strongest notes, funny songs, character songs, all the gamut, but no one, no one in the business, ever thought me capable of singing a ballad,. something I did in the Carnegie Hall Studio when I was a teenager.

I am a balladeer but I also can do the other songs quite well and that was what I was assigned.

In the later days of my stay in Virginia, I started to work on songs I loved to sing at the suggestion of Carl. I did gather quite a roster of songs which I was to use on a *One Night Only Concert* in Virginia or Washington D.C. and then we were moving and that postponed it all.

When I arrived in Pennsylvania, Pam Boyer (former editor at *Prevention Magazine*) and her husband G. Bruce Boyer (fashion writer and expert) threw a party for Carl and me to introduce us to the Lehigh Valley. It was there that I met two important people who would change the course of my life: Jeff Parks, then President of ArtsQuest/Steel Stacks and Dave Roper a wonderful pianist. Dave, I credit for bringing me out of the darkness and bringing even more to my attention my love for the story of songs.

We worked together for months, one day a week for fun. I don't remember how my first performance with Dave Roper came about…Oh, yes I do…I was trying to get another deserving talented performer booked in ArtsQuest and the demands of that artist became too much and then ArtsQuest turned to me and said "Lynnie, you take the date." I took the date the performance was successful and that led to more dates. That was the fall of 2011. Dave had a loyal following and the concert promptly sold out with curiosity about the "Little Black Girl/Woman" that was also on the bill. It was a great night, got lovely reviews and we repeated it a month or so later, but this time the audience knew my name.

Dave had done his job and then resumed his wonderful solo career which sells out audiences to this day.

After working with Dave, I worked with wonderful musicians like Ken Moyer, Kevin McConnell, Gene Perla, Tom Hamilton, Roger Latzgo, Gary Rissmiller, Lou Czechowski, Tony Marino, Don Braden, Craig Kastelink and many others. Great guys and talented musicians.

The two concerts with Dave Roper led to a series of solo concerts at the Solemme Art Gallery in Allentown then to more solo concerts at ArtsQuest and New York. I then performed at the Allentown Symphony Hall Jazz Series for Dr. Ethel Drayton-Craig and having sold that out twice and broken house records…January 23, 2016, Saturday at 7:30 PM Allentown Symphony has booked me to sing with their full orchestra…FABULOUS !

So that is where I am from not singing to singing with an orchestra. Thank you, GOD !

Lesson learned: Reinvention, renewal, vision and faith in yourself.

As I said, unique and fabulous opportunities.

More concert dates and then I introduced my vision of an Evening of Readings to ArtsQuest and my producing and directing career was launched.

I would be remiss if I did not mention my involvement as a board member on the Performing Arts Board of Arts Quest and a board Member on the organization Friends of Music. The opportunity to give back by sharing advice and experiences to these organizations enriches me at the same time.

The Project: *Unentitled.* And more.

I find that at this time in my life that I want to leave a legacy behind. My new career as a producer and director stemmed from my desire to have a place for playwrights to go to with their scripts and have a place to fail so they can succeed. An out of town try out place like New Haven, like the O'Neill Playwright's Conference. That was my dream.

Well, if you want to hear God laugh, tell God you have a plan.

I was holding auditions for the wonderful play *Unentitled* by Charles White that I was introducing to the audience at ArtsQuest. At this audition were Black actors young and old. In this atmosphere where roles for people of color are rare, the waiting room was full. When the morning people had been interviewed and worked out and proved themselves worthy of call backs, I suggested they all take a break and come back later for the call backs. They opted to stay in the creative atmosphere and talk to people that knew their plight. My gracious husband, Carl, bought most of them lunch and a bond with many actors was born. Only a few made the play, but I would call them all to tell them whether they did or not and why. I would call on one or two to participate in my next project. I would call on others to rehearse with actors on scenes. It started my core of actors.

It did occur to me there was nowhere for these actors to be nurtured like there had been for me in NEC (Negro Ensemble Company) or with Lloyd. I was blessed. So I pass it on. I want a place where new actors or underused fabulous actors can and will work. To create dedicated artists that will ultimately become stars, that is what theatre should do for the actors that work there. That is my mission, and it is evolving. With the endorsement of people I respect we are like a snowball rolling down a hill.

Here we go and where is it going to stop…I know, nobody knows…*hey, hey, hey nobody knows*…(thanks Tempting Temptations).

Update:

At the time of the above writing I was on the cusp of discovering my mission.

The successful reading of *Unentitled* by my good friend, Charles White, has cemented the opportunity to develop healthy relationships with these actors. young and not young.

My Mission: to indeed pass it on. What is *it*? The it is the knowledge, the experiences and the mentoring of these young people. As I formulate a core acting group with the help of the world renowned coach Susan Batson with many of these actors I will—through osmosis—pass through their skin follicles, the values I hope will help them after I am no longer here to physically assist. I must leave that as a legacy to the children of the theatre: Our future.

Greenwood: An American Dream Destroyed

There is another project: *Greenwood: An American Dream*

Destroyed. It sounds ominous. It is. It is about the destruction of dreams here in America at the turn of the twentieth century. Getting this play by Celeste Bedford Walker to the reading was an experience that is memorable and successful. Two successful readings one in Pennsylvania at my home base ArtsQuest and the other at the New York Theatre Workshop in Manhattan, both mind-blowing performances and received well by the audiences.

Now, mounting *Greenwood* and *Unentitled* are my goals. There is no stopping us now!

I have reinvented myself yet again, as we all must do to use up every bit of our talent.

And Yet…Tears for Change

July 16, 2015

Those who know me will say they see the optimism, the strength, the endurance and relentless persistence, in my personality. I totally agree. But every once in a while my sensitivity creeps in to be honest.

When I was working on *Greenwood*, I was looking at a video of a young actor that was submitted to me to observe his talent. He was singing an old Sam Cooke tune.

The name of the tune is *Change Gonna Come.* Those who are up on their history will note that Mr. Cooke wrote this tune in a very eventful year. His band was turned away in Shreveport, Louisiana because they were Black, his son drowned in his swimming pool, following the March on Washington and the assassination of President John F. Kennedy.

I cannot count how many times I have heard this tune and even considered to sing it myself but I never performed it. So, I listened to the song and decided to go on YouTube and listen to Mr. Cooke and a new artist L. Young sing this song.

Just to give my readers a sense of time: I had been working on the new script with the playwright Celeste Bedford Walker and was taking a break to clear my head when I decided to listen to the young man. To be clear, the script is about the life and times of the Black population of Greenwood, Oklahoma in 1921 right before, during and after the race disturbance there in Greenwood.

Now I am ready to tell you my experience. I listened to the song and as Mr. Cooke and Mr. Young sang, each time I listened to them individually sing I started to cry. I don't mean that a tear or two that might fall when the subject of race relations comes up. Oh no, I was uncontrollably sobbing, just *sobbing*. I was wondering when the ultimate "change was going to come." WHEN?

As a small child of three I was told that I said that "When I grow up prejudice will be gone" and now I talk to my friends who have grandchildren…not children but grandchildren of three years of age and the change is still coming.

Here is the story of Greenwood in 1921:

The people of Greenwood were just living out the promised American Dream that they had created for themselves and found their township was completely obliterated …destroyed… as a result of racial hatred.

I started to imagine their horror, their fear, their confusion…it was unbearable. Here I sat comfortably at my computer listening to a song and thinking of these people who had experienced what they experienced and they had sacrificed and died for my privilege to be comfortable in my home. It was unbearable. How must they have felt?

Oh, yes progress has been made. For example I am

comfortable in my home and I enjoy the privileges of an American citizen but laws cannot change attitudes. You cannot change the ignorant, confused mind of a person that insists that there are superior and inferior people. Nor can I personally persecute an entire race for individual ignorance. But when will the change come? Can we try to change one mind at a time to embrace racial harmony? When will attitudes reflect the changed laws? I don't think I will see it. The dreams of an innocent three year old child "that prejudices would be gone when I grow up"… I fear that racial hatred disappearing is just that a dream, a dream that I will not realize in my lifetime.

My heart aches and breaks for those people whose lives were sacrificed for my freedom… in the past and present.

So the tears I shed that night and those tears I will shed in the future. I shed for those who made it possible for me to freely write about my dream, my hope, for those three year olds of today! Maybe they will see it.

Conversations with a Protected Child

One might wonder about the title of my first foray into dialogue through the social media…What is a "protected" child?

Well, let me explain as much as I as can. As a child of my generation, a child of the "the greatest generation," I was protected from the vicious, venomous reaches of racism by two parents who employed the tactics of a military general.

I was an adult on the set of the *704 Hauser* before I discovered I was protected. There was an episode that never aired which discussed the ways Black parents of the 1940s, 1950s and even 1960s sheltered their children from the indignities of racism. It hit me on a show break that my parents had practiced this and I was never aware of it. Sadly my father had passed away months before; however my mother was still alive. I rushed to the phone and posed the question to my sweet ailing, fiery mother. "Mom, did you create picnics and events on our trips to protect me from thinking or finding out that I was not...we were not welcome somewhere?" There was a silence and then an uncharacteristic "Uh huh" with a slight break in her voice. Tears immediately came to my eyes, for I know that even then my mother never wanted me to think I was not allowed to do anything any other child could do. She was still protecting me.

Then a rush of memories came to my mind that over those formative years where My Mother and her friends... Black and White had protected me from the harsh stares and whispers.

I will recall one event: My mother's Jewish friend and customer Rhoda Lipoff of Englewood, New Jersey invited me with her daughters Lisa and Laurie (I think Laurie was home that day) to swim in the building pool downstairs. I remember my mother's funny hesitancy to have me participate. I thought "Oh, she's afraid, because I really don't know how to swim." She needn't have worried about my swimming safety or my getting my hair wet because I was never going out of the shallow water and never putting my newly pressed hair under water....

But what my mother knew was that some of the women in that building—even though they themselves were the product of racism at its worse decades before—they had no desire to have their pool shared with any child that did share their same color unless the child's parents were celebrities...maybe.

My mother's friend assuaged her fears by saying, "Oh no worries. I am going down with the girls." I remember the stern looks displayed and then the way those same looks vanished as the overpowering presence (silently, of course) of Rhoda, who made it perfectly clear she was ready to confront each and every one of them and their husbands if a moment of discomfort occurred. I saw it but paid no attention. I never thought it had to do with me. I was truly a product of childhood naiveté.

How I wish today I could hug and kiss both of these ladies for their bravery and love. That is not to be, for my mother passed away in 1996 and her friend Rhoda is still alive but is now the victim of Alzheimer's. As her loving family surrounds her; she recognizes none of them. My hug and kiss would go unrecognized.

Yes, as I recall these stories I know there are countless more that can be discussed and recorded. SO here is my point: I was protected as a child, now it is my turn to protect, if it is wanted or not.

My husband, Carl is a mathematical genius in his own right, but has no patience or very little patience. When he decided to tutor children in our area, I thought, "Oh. my." But he returned home from his first session, exuberant, talkative and concerned but not inpatient. His concern was that most of the children in this lovely program were without fundamentals. You know those things that teach reasoning and deduction in life. The children did not know their multiplication tables. Now as any adult should be able to tell you, multiplication tables are memorization, but they teach us other things. They teach how to reach solutions, deductions, reasoning etc. Our children are entering our society and are not equipped to deal with the challenges. Why? Many reasons.

Budget cuts, no job incentives given to teachers. But what is our solution. I can type here and type a number of reasons. We need solutions. Let us protect our children as we were protected…ALL our children… All COLORS AND RACES… to rephrase a Beatle tune…

HELP! We need somebody

Please just everybody…HELP!

My on-going experience with *Greenwood* makes me realize that we must speak up NOW, that later on is too late.

So, I invite a conversation…from those of you on line…teachers, parents, insightful adults…Where do we go from here?

Let us find some solutions

Let us have a conversation….share some of your protection stories.

But let us not just talk, let's mobilize! Let us find an answer for the CHILDREN!!!!

Write me on twitter @ #lynniegodfrey, video conversation with me on Instagram or Tumble on @lynniegodfrey.

CLOSING NOTE

I didn't want to end my journey with you, my reader, without making it clear my objectives in writing this guide.

It is quite simple: *JUST KEEP TRYING...*

No matter if you are a frustrated teacher in a system that long since stopped listening to your needs to educate and care for our wonderful children, or a college student who might not fit in socially or fit in too well and forgot about the academics...pick it up and start again...make it work. You can.

You might be a corporate executive whose personality clashed with the "in crowd" at the time. Wait awhile. Maybe the old stuffed shirts will retire or move on, but don't give up.

Or, God help you, if you are a young struggling performer or—Blessings! —an older performer hanging in there...Please keep trying...don't give up the dream.

I think we sometimes get what we want and more often times get what we need but no matter what, we still have to *TRY*...to get it. I have been referred to as, compliment or not, "The ever ready bunny." I keep going, keep reinventing. We all must do that in all professions, and why not?

Nothing, I mean nothing, beats a try. Failure is not an option. To fail is simply not to try. Your mentors have told you that. So if you get nothing from this guide, know I am still trying and will continue to try until I am no longer here and I will be looking for you on that same road whether it be yellow brick or not.

Please take this simple thought away with you as you close the pages to this guide. I will look for you down the road and remember... *We may not get everything thing we want but why not try for it all!*

JUST KEEP TRYING.

Just because you're not a megastar doesn't mean you are not a success. But doing nothing, guarantees you are a failure.

Maestro, Take it From the Top!

Here I am, performer, director, producer...All in one fell swoop. It is a wonderful place to be but it is not without its challenges and disappointments.

Look at the future. There are many things to be achieved. My devotion to family members was always first but now that the last member of my nuclear family, my primary concern, is gone (my dear Jo-Ann) I will work on my goals and look always to the heavens for the support of my blood family whom I miss everyday ... every minute!

Yes, I am home...back in the Northeast with frequent trips to Los Angeles which I hope will kindle fun connections for the plays and me. Only the future will tell. Maybe that will be in another book: A follow-up to what happens on this new journey and what the actors and I have learned.

Love you madly,

Lynnie Godfrey

About the Author

Lynnie Godfrey received a *Drama Desk* nomination for her Broadway debut performance in the Musical Revue *EUBIE!* For excellence in Directing she is the recipient of the Tyrone Guthrie Award as well as the NAACP Award for Producing. She received the DRAMALOGUE and NAACP Awards for Outstanding Performance by a Supporting Actress for her portrayal in *No Place To Be Somebody*. The AUDELCO Award was given to her for outstanding performance in *Shuffle Along*. For her recording performance of *Snow Queen*, she received both the Audio Earphone and Benjamin Franklin Awards. Grammy recognition was received for her recent CDs...*Lynnie Godfrey Does It Her Way* and *Spending The Holiday With Lynnie Godfrey*.

Other theatre performances include: Lola in *Damn Yankees* during a record breaking run at Hartford Stage, James Weldon Johnson's *God's Trombones*, August Wilson's *Gem Of The Ocean* at Arena Stage, *Three Penny Opera* as Jenny Diver at ESIPA, Christopher Durang's *Nature And Purpose Of The Universe* and many more.

Ms. Godfrey's film credits include the Disney Detective film: *V.I. Warshawski* as Sal, the best friend of Kathleen Turner. In television she starred in the CBS/ Norman Lear sequel to *All In The Family* ...*704 Hauser*. More than 30

Television guest and recurring appearances include: *LA Law, Amen, 227, Frank's Place* as well as in Oprah Winfrey's series *The Women Of Brewster Place.*

Ms. Godfrey sits on the Board of Friends of Music and is a member of the Performing Arts Board at ArtsQuest. She is President and CEO of GodLee Entertainment, Inc. her production company, which seeks new works to develop and to produce.

She enjoys working closely with playwright, Celeste Bedford Walker on the script of *Greenwood: An American Dream Destroyed.* The debut reading of this play took place at ArtsQuest Performing Arts Center followed by a New York City reading at The New York Workshop Theatre. This is the second play reading directed by Ms. Godfrey in the Lehigh Valley this season. The first play was *Unentitled* by the talented Charles White, which was successfully received by ArtsQuest audiences and read at the Susan Batson Studios in New York City.

Ms. Godfrey is scheduled to direct a reading of *Lois's Wedding*, a play by Bathsheba Monk on March 21, 2016 at ArtsQuest.

This is Ms. Godfrey's first book.

www.ingramcontent.com/pod-product-compliance
Lightning Source LLC
LaVergne TN
LVHW051425080426
835508LV00022B/3239